T0205022

ENCOUNTER
ON THE
SEINE

OTHER BOOKS IN THE
JAMES BALDWIN CENTENNIAL SERIES

Everybody's Protest Novel

Harlem Ghetto

OTHER WORKS BY JAMES BALDWIN

Notes of a Native Son

Jimmy's Blues and Other Poems

Nothing Personal

ENCOUNTER ON THE SEINE

Essays

JAMES BALDWIN

BEACON PRESS
BOSTON

BEACON PRESS
Boston, Massachusetts
www.beacon.org

Beacon Press books
are published under the auspices of
the Unitarian Universalist Association of Congregations.

27 26 25 24   8 7 6 5 4 3 2 1

This book is printed on acid-free paper that meets
the uncoated paper ANSI/NISO specifications for
permanence as revised in 1992.

Author photo by Carl Van Vechten, printed with permission
of the Van Vechten Trust and acquired from the Beinecke
Rare Book and Manuscript Library, Yale University.

Text design and composition by Kim Arney

*Library of Congress Cataloging-in-Publication
Data is available for this title.*
ISBN: 978-0-8070-1867-5; e-book: 978-0-8070-1868-2

CONTENTS

ENCOUNTER ON
THE SEINE

Black Meets Brown

IN PARIS NOWADAYS it is rather more difficult for an American Negro to become a really successful entertainer than it is rumored to have been some thirty years ago. For one thing, champagne has ceased to be drunk out of slippers, and the frivolously colored thousand-franc note is neither as elastic nor as freely spent as it was in the 1920's. The musicians and singers who are here now must work very hard indeed to acquire the polish and style which will land them in the big time. Bearing witness to this eternally tantalizing possibility, performers whose eminence is unchallenged, like Duke Ellington or Louis Armstrong, occasionally pass through. Some of their ambitious followers are in or near the big time already; others are gaining reputations which have yet to be tested in the States. Gordon Heath, who will be remembered for his performances as the embattled soldier in Broadway's *Deep Are the Roots* some seasons back, sings ballads nightly in his own night club on the Rue L'Abbaye; and everyone who comes to Paris these days sooner or later discovers Chez Inez, a night club in the Latin Quarter run by a singer named Inez Cavanaugh, which specializes in fried chicken and jazz. It is at Chez Inez that many an unknown first performs in public, going on thereafter, if not always to greater triumphs, at least to other night clubs, and possibly landing a contract to tour the Riviera during the spring and summer.

In general, only the Negro entertainers are able to maintain a useful and unquestioning comradeship with other Negroes. Their non-performing, colored countrymen are, nearly to a man, incomparably more isolated, and it must be conceded that this isolation is deliberate. It is estimated that there are five hundred American Negroes living in this city, the vast majority of them veterans studying on the G.I. Bill. They are studying everything from the Sorbonne's standard *Cours de Civilisation Française* to abnormal psychology, brain surgery, music, fine arts, and literature. Their isolation from each other is not difficult to understand if one bears in mind the axiom, unquestioned by American landlords, that Negroes are happy only when they are kept together. Those driven to break this pattern by leaving the U.S. ghettos not merely have effected a social and physical leave-taking but also have been precipitated into cruel psychological warfare. It is altogether inevitable that past humiliations should become associated not only with one's traditional oppressors but also with one's traditional kinfolk.

Thus the sight of a face from home is not invariably a source of joy, but can also quite easily become a source of embarrassment or rage. The American Negro in Paris is forced at last to exercise an undemocratic discrimination rarely practiced by Americans, that of judging his people, duck by duck, and distinguishing them one from another. Through this deliberate isolation, through lack of numbers, and above all through his own overwhelming need to be, as it were, forgotten, the American Negro in Paris is very nearly the invisible man.

The wariness with which he regards his colored kin is a natural extension of the wariness with which he regards all of his countrymen. At the beginning, certainly, he cherishes rather exaggerated hopes of the French. His white countrymen, by and large, fail to justify his fears, partly because the social climate does not encourage an outward display of racial bigotry, partly out of their awareness of being ambassadors, and finally, I should think, because they are themselves relieved at being no longer forced to think in terms of color. There remains, nevertheless, in the encounter of white Americans and Negro Americans the high potential of an awkward or an ugly situation.

The white American regards his darker brother through the distorting screen created by a lifetime of conditioning. He is accustomed to regard him either as a needy and deserving martyr or as the soul of rhythm, but he is more than a little intimidated to find this stranger so many miles from home. At first he tends instinctively, whatever his intelligence may belatedly clamor, to take it as a reflection on his personal honor and good-will; and at the same time, with that winning generosity, at once good-natured and uneasy, which characterizes Americans, he would like to establish communication, and sympathy, with his compatriot. "And how do *you* feel about it?" he would like to ask, "it" being anything—the Russians, Betty Grable, the Place de la Concorde. The trouble here is that any "it," so tentatively offered, may suddenly become loaded and vibrant with tension, creating in the air between the two thus met an intolerable atmosphere of danger.

The Negro, on the other hand, via the same conditioning which constricts the outward gesture of the whites, has learned to anticipate: as the mouth opens he divines what the tongue will utter. He has had time, too, long before he came to Paris, to reflect on the absolute and personally expensive futility of taking any one of his countrymen to task for his status in America, or of hoping to convey to them any of his experience. The American Negro and white do not, therefore, discuss the past, except in considerately guarded snatches. Both are quite willing, and indeed quite wise, to remark instead the considerably overrated impressiveness of the Eiffel Tower.

The Eiffel Tower has naturally long since ceased to divert the French, who consider that all Negroes arrive from America, trumpet-laden and twinkle-toed, bearing scars so unutterably painful that all of the glories of the French Republic may not suffice to heal them. This indignant generosity poses problems of its own, which, language and custom being what they are, are not so easily averted.

The European tends to avoid the really monumental confusion which might result from an attempt to apprehend the relationship of the forty-eight states to one another, clinging instead to such information as is afforded by radio, press, and film, to anecdotes considered to be illustrative of American life, and to the myth that we have ourselves perpetuated. The result, in conversation, is rather like seeing one's back yard reproduced with extreme fidelity, but in such a perspective that it becomes a place which one has never seen or visited, which never has existed, and which never can exist. The Negro is forced to say "Yes" to many a difficult question, and yet to deny the conclusion to which his answers seem to point. His past, he now realizes, has not been simply a series of ropes and bonfires and humiliations, but something vastly more complex, which, as he thinks painfully, "It was much worse than that," was also, he irrationally feels, something much better. As it is useless to excoriate his countrymen, it is galling now to be pitied as a victim, to accept this ready sympathy which is limited only by its failure to accept him as an American. He finds himself involved, in another language, in the same old battle: the battle for his own identity. To accept the reality of his being an American becomes a matter involving his integrity and his greatest hopes, for only by accepting this reality can he hope to make articulate to himself or to others the uniqueness of his experience, and to set free the spirit so long anonymous and caged.

The ambivalence of his status is thrown into relief by his encounters with the Negro students from France's colonies who live in Paris. The French African comes from a region and a way of life which—at least from the American point of view—is exceedingly primitive, and where exploitation takes more naked forms. In Paris, the African Negro's status, conspicuous and subtly inconvenient, is that of a colonial; and he leads here the intangibly precarious life of someone abruptly and recently uprooted. His bitterness is unlike that of his American kinsman in that it is not so treacherously likely to be turned against himself. He has, not so very many miles away, a homeland to which his relationship, no less than his responsibility, is overwhelmingly clear: His country must be given—or it must seize—its freedom. This bitter ambition is shared by his fellow colonials, with whom he has a common language, and whom he has no wish whatever to avoid; without whose sustenance, indeed, he would be almost altogether lost in Paris. They live in groups together, in the same neighborhoods, in student hotels and under conditions which cannot fail to impress the American as almost unendurable.

Yet what the American is seeing is not simply the poverty of the student but the enormous gap between the European and American standards of living. *All* of the students in the Latin Quarter live in ageless, sinister-looking hotels; they are all forced continually to choose between cigarettes and cheese at lunch.

It is true that the poverty and anger which the American Negro sees must be related to Europe and not to America. Yet, as he wishes for a moment that he were home again, where at least the terrain is familiar, there begins to race within him, like the despised beat of the tom-tom, echoes of a past which he has not yet been able to utilize, intimations of a responsibility which he has not yet been able to face. He begins to conjecture how much he has gained and lost during his long sojourn in the American republic. The African before him has endured privation, injustice, medieval cruelty; but the African has not yet endured the utter alienation of himself from his people and his past. His mother did not sing "Sometimes I Feel Like a Motherless Child," and he has not, all his life long, ached for acceptance in a culture which pronounced straight hair and white skin the only acceptable beauty.

They face each other, the Negro and the African, over a gulf of three hundred years—an alienation too vast to be conquered in an evening's good-will, too heavy and too double-edged ever to be trapped in speech. This alienation causes the Negro to recognize that he is a hybrid. Not a physical hybrid merely: in every aspect of his living he betrays the memory of the auction block and the impact of the happy ending. In white Americans he finds reflected—repeated, as it were, in a higher key—his tensions, his terrors, his tenderness. Dimly and for the first time, there begins to fall into perspective the nature of the roles they have played in the lives and history of each other. Now he is bone of their bone, flesh of their flesh; they have loved and hated and obsessed and feared each other and his blood is in their soil. Therefore he cannot deny them, nor can they ever be divorced.

The American Negro cannot explain to the African what surely seems in himself to be a want of manliness, of racial pride, a maudlin ability to forgive. It is difficult to make clear that he is not seeking to forfeit his birthright as a black man, but that, on the contrary, it is precisely this birthright which he is struggling to recognize and make articulate. Perhaps it now occurs to him that in this need to establish himself in relation to his past he is most American, that this depthless alienation from oneself and one's people is, in sum, the American experience.

Yet one day he will face his home again; nor can he realistically expect to find overwhelming changes. In America, it is true, the appearance is perpetually changing, each generation greeting with short-lived exultation yet more dazzling additions to our renowned façade. But the ghetto, anxiety, bitterness, and guilt continue to breed their indescribable complex of tensions. What time will bring Americans is at last their own identity. It is on this dangerous voyage and in the same boat that the American Negro will make peace with himself and with the voiceless many thousands gone before him.

A QUESTION
OF IDENTITY

THE AMERICAN STUDENT COLONY in Paris is a social phenomenon so amorphous as to at once demand and defy the generality. One is far from being in the position of finding not enough to say—one finds far too much, and everything one finds is contradictory. What one wants to know at bottom, is what *they* came to find: to which question there are—at least—as many answers as there are faces at the café tables.

The assumed common denominator, which is their military experience, does not shed on this question as much light as one might hope. For one thing, it becomes impossible, the moment one thinks about it, to predicate the existence of a *common* experience. The moment one thinks about it, it becomes apparent that there is no such thing. That experience is a private, and a very largely speechless affair is the principal truth, perhaps, to which the colony under discussion bears witness—though the aggressively unreadable face which they, collectively, present also suggests the more disturbing possibility that experience may perfectly well be meaningless. This loaded speculation aside, it is certainly true that whatever this experience has done to them, or for them, whatever the effect has been, is, or will be, is a question to which no one has yet given any strikingly coherent answer. Military experience does not, furthermore, necessarily mean experience of battle, so that the student colony's common denominator reduces itself to nothing more than the fact that all of its members have spent some time in uniform. This is the common denominator of their entire generation, of which the majority is not to be found in Paris, or, for that matter, in Europe. One is at the outset, therefore, forbidden to assume that the fact of having surrendered to the necessary anonymity of uniform, or of having undergone the shock of battle, was enough to occasion this flight from home. The best that one can do by way of uniting these so disparate identities is simply to accept, without comment, the fact of their military experience, without questioning its extent; and, further, to suggest that they form, by virtue of their presence here, a somewhat unexpected minority. Unlike the majority of their fellows, who were simply glad to get back home, these have elected to tarry in the Old World, among scenes and people unimaginably removed from anything they have known. They are willing, apparently, at least for a season, to endure the wretched Parisian plumbing, the public baths, the Paris age, and dirt—to pursue some end, mysterious and largely inarticulate, arbitrarily summed up in the verb *to study*.

Arbitrarily, because, however hard the ex-GI is studying, it is very difficult to believe that it was only for this reason that he traveled so far. He is not, usually, studying anything which he couldn't study at home, in far greater comfort. (We are limiting ourselves, for the moment, to those people who are—more or less seriously—studying, as opposed to those, to be considered later, who are merely gold-bricking.) The people, for example, who are studying painting, which seems, until one looks around, the best possible subject to be studying here, are not studying, after all, with Picasso, or Matisse—they are studying with teachers of the same caliber as those they would have found in the States. They are treated by these teachers with the same highhandedness, and they accept their dicta with the very same measure of American salt. Nor can it be said that they produce canvases of any greater interest than those to be found along Washington Square, or in the cold-water flats of New York's lower east side. There is, *au contraire*, more than a little truth to the contention that the east side has a certain edge over Montparnasse, and this in spite of the justly renowned Paris light. If we tentatively use—purely by virtue of his numbers—the student painter as the nearest possible approach to a "typical" student, we find that his motives for coming to Paris are anything but clear. One is forced to suppose that it was nothing more than the legend of Paris, not infrequently at its most vulgar and superficial level. It was certainly no love for French tradition, whatever, indeed, in his mind, that tradition may be; and, in any case, since he is himself without a tradition, he is ill equipped to deal with the traditions of any other people. It was no love for their language, which he doesn't, beyond the most inescapable necessities, speak; nor was it any love for their history, his grasp of French history being yet more feeble than his understanding of his own. It was no love for the monuments, cathedrals, palaces, shrines, for which, again, nothing in his experience prepares him, and to which, when he is not totally indifferent, he brings only the hurried bewilderment of the tourist. It was not even any particular admiration, or sympathy for the French, or, at least, none strong enough to bear the strain of actual contact. He may, at home, have admired their movies, in which case, confronting the reality, he tends to feel a little taken in. Those images created by Marcel Carné, for example, prove themselves treacherous precisely because they are so exact. The sordid French hotel room, so admirably detailed by the camera, speaking, in its quaintness, and distance, so beautifully of romance, undergoes a sea-change, becomes a room positively hostile to romance, once it is oneself, and not Jean Gabin, who lives there. This is the difference, simply, between what one desires and what the reality insists on—which difference we will not pursue except to observe that, since the reasons which brought the student here are so romantic, and incoherent, he has come, in effect, to a city which exists only in his mind. He cushions himself, so it would seem, against the shock of reality, by refusing for a very long time to recognize Paris at all, but clinging instead to its image. This is the reason, perhaps, that Paris for so long fails to make any mark on him; and may also be why, when the tension between the real and the imagined can no longer be supported, so many people undergo a species of breakdown, or take the first boat home.

For Paris is, according to its legend, the city where everyone loses his head, and his morals, lives through at least one *histoire d'amour*, ceases, quite, to arrive anywhere on time, and thumbs his nose at the Puritans—the city, in brief, where all become drunken on the fine old air of freedom. This legend, in the fashion of legends, has this much to support it, that it is not at all difficult to see how it got started. It is limited, as legends are limited, by being—literally—unlivable, and by referring to the past. It is perhaps not amazing, therefore, that this legend appears to have virtually nothing to do with the life of Paris itself, with the lives, that is, of the natives, to whom the city, no less than the legend, belong. The charm of this legend proves itself capable of withstanding the most improbable excesses of the French bureaucracy, the weirdest vagaries of the *concierge*, the fantastic rents paid for uncomfortable apartments, the discomfort itself, and, even, the great confusion and despair which is reflected in French politics—and in French faces. More, the legend operates to place all of the inconveniences endured by the foreigner, to say nothing of the downright misery which is the lot of many of the natives, in the gentle glow of the picturesque, and the absurd; so that, finally, it is perfectly possible to be enamored of Paris while remaining totally indifferent, or even hostile to the French. And this is made possible by the one person in Paris whom the legend seems least to affect, who is not living it at all, that is, the Parisian himself. He, with his impenetrable *politesse*, and with techniques unspeakably more direct, keeps the traveler at an unmistakable arm's length. Unlucky indeed, as well as rare, the traveler who thirsts to know the lives of the people—the people don't want him in their lives. Neither does the Parisian exhibit the faintest personal interest, or curiosity, concerning the life, or habits, of any stranger. So long as he keeps within the law, which, after all, most people have sufficient ingenuity to do, he may stand on his head, for all the Parisian cares. It is this arrogant indifference on the part of the Parisian, with its unpredictable effects on the traveler, which makes so splendid the Paris air, to say nothing whatever of the exhilarating effect it has on the Paris scene.

The American student lives here, then, in a kind of social limbo. He is allowed, and he gratefully embraces irresponsibility; and, at the same time, since he is an American, he is invested with power, whether or not he likes it, however he may choose to confirm or deny it. Though the students of any nation, in Paris, are allowed irresponsibility, few seem to need it as desperately as Americans seem to need it; and none, naturally, move in the same aura of power, which sets up in the general breast a perceptible anxiety, and wonder, and a perceptible resentment. This is the "catch," for the American, in the Paris freedom: that he becomes here a kind of revenant to Europe, the future of which continent, it may be, is in his hands. The problems proceeding from the distinction he thus finds thrust upon him might not, for a sensibility less definitively lonely, frame so painful a dilemma: but the American wishes to be liked *as a person*, an implied distinction which makes perfect sense to him, and none whatever to the European. What the American means is that he does not want to be confused with the Marshall Plan, Hollywood, the Yankee dollar, television, or Senator McCarthy. What the European, in a thoroughly exasperating innocence, assumes is that the American cannot, of course, be divorced from the so diverse phenomena which make up his country, and that he is willing, and able, to clarify the American conundrum. If the American cannot do this, his despairing aspect seems to say, who, under heaven, can? This moment, which instinctive ingenuity delays as long as possible, nevertheless arrives, and punctuates the Paris honeymoon. It is the moment, so to speak, when one leaves the Paris of legend and finds oneself in the real and difficult Paris of the present. At this moment Paris ceases to be a city dedicated to *la vie bohème*, and becomes one of the cities of Europe. At this point, too, it may be suggested, the legend of Paris has done its deadly work, which is, perhaps, so to stun the traveler with freedom that he begins to long for the prison of home——home then becoming the place where questions are not asked.

It is at this point, precisely, that many and many a student packs his bags for home. The transformation which can be effected, in less than a year, in the attitude and aspirations of the youth who has divorced himself from the crudities of main street in order to be married with European finesse is, to say the very least, astounding. His brief period of enchantment having ended, he cannot wait, it seems, to look again on his native land——the virtues of which, if not less crude, have also become, abruptly, *simple*, and *vital*. With the air of a man who has but barely escaped tumbling headlong into the bottomless pit, he tells you that he can scarcely

wait to leave this city, which has been revealed to
the eye of his maturity as old, dirty, crumbling,
and dead. The people who were, when he arrived
at Le Havre, the heirs of the world's richest culture, the possessors of the world's largest *esprit*,
are really decadent, penurious, self-seeking, and
false, with no trace of American spontaneity, and
lacking in the least gratitude for American favors.
Only America is alive, only Americans are doing
anything worth mentioning in the arts, or in any
other field of human activity: to America, only,
the future belongs. Whereas, but only yesterday,
to confess a fondness for anything American was to
be suspected of the most indefensible jingoism, to
suggest today that Europe is not all black is to place
oneself under the suspicion of harboring trea-
sonable longings. The violence of his embrace of
things American is embarrassing, not only because
one is not quite prepared to follow his admirable
example, but also because it is impossible not to

suspect that his present acceptance of his country is no less romantic, and unreal, than his earlier rejection. It is as easy, after all, and as meaning-less, to embrace uncritically the cultural sterility of main street as it is to decry it. Both extremes avoid the question of whether or not main street is really sterile, avoid, in fact—which is the principal convenience of extremes—any questions about main street at all. What one vainly listens for in this cacophony of affirmation is any echo, how-ever faint of individual maturity. It is really quite impossible to be affirmative about anything which one refuses to question; one is doomed to remain inarticulate about anything which one hasn't, by an act of the imagination, made one's own. This so suddenly affirmative student is but changing the fashion of his innocence, nothing being more improbable than that he is now prepared, as he insists, to embrace his Responsibilities—the very word, in the face of his monumental aversion to experience, seems to shrink to the dimensions of a new, and rather sinister, frivolity.

The student, homeward bound, has only chosen, however, to flee down the widest road. Of those who remain here, the majority have taken roads more devious, and incomparably better hidden— so well hidden that they themselves are lost.

One very often finds in this category that student whose adaptation to French life seems to have been most perfect, and whose studies—of French art, or the drama, the language, or the history—give him the greatest right to be here. This student has put aside chewing gum forever, he eschews the T-shirt, and the crew cut, he can only with difficulty be prevailed upon to see an American movie, and it is so patent that he is *actually* studying that his appearance at the café tables is never taken as evidence of frivolity, but only as proof of his admirable passion to study the customs

of the country. One assumes that he is living as
the French live—which assumption, however, is
immediately challenged by the suspicion that no
American can live as the French live, even if one
could find an American who wanted to. This student lives, nevertheless, with a French family, with
whom he speaks French, and takes his meals; and
he knows, as some students do not, that the Place
de la Bastille no longer holds the prison. He has
read, or is reading, all of Racine, Proust, Gide,
Sartre, and authors more obscure—in the orig-
inal, naturally. He regularly visits the museums,
and he considers Arletty to be the most beautiful
woman and the finest actress in the world. But the
world, it seems, has become the French world:
he is unwilling to recognize any other. This so se-
verely cramps the American conversational style,
that one looks on this student with awe, and some
shame—he is so spectacularly getting out of his
European experience everything it has to give. He

has certainly made contact with the French, and isn't wasting his time in Paris talking to people he might perfectly well have met in America. His friends are French, in the classroom, in the bistro, on the boulevard, and, of course, at home—it is only that one is sometimes driven to wonder what on earth they find to talk about. This wonder is considerably increased when, in the rare conversations he condescends to have in English, one discovers that, certain picturesque details aside, he seems to know no more about life in Paris than everybody knew at home. His friends have, it appears, leaped unscathed from the nineteenth into the twentieth century, entirely undismayed by any of the reverses suffered by their country. This makes them a remarkable band indeed, but it is in vain that one attempts to discover anything more about them—their conversation being limited, one gathers, to remarks about French wine, witticisms concerning l'amour, French history, and the glories of Paris. The remarkably limited range of their minds is matched only by their perplexing definition of friendship, a definition which does not seem to include any suggestion of communication, still less of intimacy. Since, in short, the relationship of this perfectly adapted student to the people he now so strenuously adores is based simply on his unwillingness to allow them any of the human attributes with which his countrymen so confounded him at home, and since his vaunted grasp of their history reveals itself as the merest academic platitude, involving his imagination not at all, the extent of his immersion in French life impresses one finally as the height of artificiality, and, even, of presumption. The most curious thing about the passion with which he has embraced the Continent is that it seems to be nothing more or less than a means of safeguarding his American simplicity. He has placed himself in a kind of strongbox of custom, and refuses to see anything in Paris which can't be seen through a golden haze. He is thus protected against reality, or experience, or change, and has succeeded in placing beyond the reach of corruption values he prefers not to examine. Even his multitudinous French friends help him to do this, for it is impossible, after all, to be friends with a mob: they are simply a cloud of faces, bearing witness to romance.

Between these two extremes, the student who embraces Home, and the student who embraces The Continent—both embraces, as we have tried to indicate, being singularly devoid of contact, to say nothing of love—there are far more gradations than can be suggested here. The American in Europe is everywhere confronted with the question of his identity, and this may be taken as the key to all the contradictions one encounters when attempting to discuss him. Certainly, for the student colony one finds no other common denominator—this is all, really, that they have in common, and they are distinguished from each other by the ways in which they come to terms, or fail to come to terms with their confusion. This prodigious question, at home so little recognized, seems, germ-like, to be vivified in the European air, and to grow disproportionately, displacing previous assurances, and producing tensions and bewilderments entirely unlooked for. It is not, moreover, a question which limits itself to those who are, so to speak, in traffic with ideas. It confronts everyone, finding everyone unprepared; it is a question with implications not easily escaped, and the attempt to escape can precipitate disaster. Our perfectly adapted student, for example, should his strongbox of custom break, may find himself hurled into that coterie of gold-bricks who form such a spectacular element of the Paris scene that they are often what the Parisian has in the foreground of his mind when he wonderingly mutters,

C'est vraiment les Américains. The great majority of this group, having attempted, on more or less personal levels, to lose or disguise their antecedents, are reduced to a kind of rubble of compulsion. Having cast off all previous disciplines, they have also lost the shape which these disciplines made for them and have not succeeded in finding any other. Their rejection of the limitations of American society has not set them free to function in any other society, and their illusions, therefore, remain intact: they have yet to be corrupted by the notion that society is never anything less than a perfect labyrinth of limitations. They are charmed by the reflection that Paris is more than two thousand years old, but it escapes them that the Parisian has been in the making just about that long, and that one does not, therefore, become Parisian by virtue of a Paris address. This little band of bohemians, as grimly singleminded as any evangelical sect, illustrate, by the very ferocity with which they disavow

American attitudes, one of the most American of attributes, the inability to believe that time is real. It is this inability which makes them so romantic about the nature of society, and it is this inability which has led them into a total confusion about the nature of experience. Society, it would seem, is a flimsy structure, beneath contempt, designed by and for all the other people, and experience is nothing more than sensation—so many sensations, added up like arithmetic, give one the rich, full life. They thus lose what it was they so bravely set out to find, their own personalities, which, having been deprived of all nourishment, soon cease, in effect, to exist; and they arrive, finally, at a dangerous disrespect for the personalities of others. Though they persist in believing that their present shapelessness is freedom, it is observable that this present freedom is unable to endure either silence or privacy, and demands, for its ultimate expression, a rootless wandering among the cafés. Saint Germain des Près, the heart of the American colony, so far from having absorbed the American student, has been itself transformed, on spring, summer, and fall nights, into a replica, very nearly, of Times Square.

But if this were all one found in the American student colony, one would hardly have the heart to discuss it. If the American found in Europe only confusion, it would obviously be infinitely wiser for him to remain at home. Hidden, however, in the heart of the confusion he encounters here is that which he came so blindly seeking: the terms on which he is related to his country, and to the world. This, which has so grandiose and general a ring, is, in fact, most personal—the American confusion seeming to be based on the very nearly unconscious assumption that it is possible to consider the person apart from all the forces which have produced him. This assumption, however, is itself based on nothing less than our history, which is the history of the total, and willing, alienation of entire peoples from their forebears. What is overwhelmingly clear, it seems, to everyone but ourselves is that this history has created an entirely unprecedented people, with a unique and individual past. It is, indeed, this past which has thrust upon us our present, so troubling role. It is the past lived on the American continent, as against that other past, irrecoverable now on the shores of Europe, which must sustain us in the present. The truth about that past is not that it is too brief, or too superficial, but only that we, having turned our faces so resolutely away from it, have never demanded from it what it has to give. It is this demand which the American student in Paris is forced, at length, to make, for he has otherwise no identity, no reason for being here, nothing to sustain him here. From the vantage point of Europe he discovers his own country. And this is a discovery which not only brings to an end the alienation of the American from himself, but which also makes clear to him, for the first time, the extent of his involvement in the life of Europe.

EQUAL IN PARIS

O<small>N THE 19TH OF DECEMBER</small>, in 1949, when I had been living in Paris for a little over a year, I was arrested as a receiver of stolen goods and spent eight days in prison. My arrest came about through an American tourist whom I had met twice in New York, who had been given my name and address and told to look me up. I was then living on the top floor of a ludicrously grim hotel on the rue du Bac, one of those enormous dark, cold, and hideous establishments in which Paris abounds that seem to breathe forth, in their airless, humid, stone-cold halls, the weak light,

scurrying chambermaids, and creaking stairs, an
odor of gentility long long dead. The place was
run by an ancient Frenchman dressed in an elegant
black suit which was green with age, who cannot
properly be described as bewildered or even as being in a state of shock, since he had really stopped
breathing around 1910. There he sat at his desk in
the weirdly lit, fantastically furnished lobby, day
in and day out, greeting each one of his extremely
impoverished and *louche* lodgers with a stately inclination of the head that he had no doubt been
taught in some impossibly remote time was the
proper way for a propriétaire to greet his guests.
If it had not been for his daughter, an extremely
hardheaded tricoteuse—the inclination of her
head was chilling and abrupt, like the downbeat
of an ax—the hotel would certainly have gone
bankrupt long before. It was said that this old man
had not gone farther than the door of his hotel
for thirty years, which was not at all difficult to

believe. He looked as though the daylight would have killed him.

I did not, of course, spend much of my time in this palace. The moment I began living in French hotels I understood the necessity of French cafés. This made it rather difficult to look me up, for as soon as I was out of bed I hopefully took notebook and fountain pen off to the upstairs room of the Flore, where I consumed rather a lot of coffee and, as evening approached, rather a lot of alcohol, but did not get much writing done. But one night, in one of the cafés of St. Germain des Près, I was discovered by this New Yorker and only because we found ourselves in Paris we immediately established the illusion that we had been fast friends back in the good old U.S.A. This illusion proved itself too thin to support an evening's drinking, but by that time it was too late. I had committed myself to getting him a room in my hotel the next day, for he was living in one of the nest of hotels near the Gare St. Lazare, where, he said, the *propriétaire* was a thief, his wife a repressed nymphomaniac, the chambermaids "pigs," and the rent a crime. Americans are always talking this way about the French and so it did not occur to me that he meant what he said or that he would take into his own hands the means of avenging himself on the French Republic. It did not occur to me, either, that the means which he did take could possibly have brought about such dire results, results which were not less dire for being also comic-opera.

It came as the last of a series of disasters which had perhaps been made inevitable by the fact that I had come to Paris originally with a little over forty dollars in my pockets, nothing in the bank, and no grasp whatever of the French language. It developed, shortly, that I had no grasp of the French character either. I considered the French an ancient, intelligent, and cultured race, which indeed they are. I did not know, however, that ancient glories imply, at least in the middle of the present century, present fatigue and, quite probably, paranoia; that there is a limit to the role of the intelligence in human affairs; and that no people come into possession of a culture without having paid a heavy price for it. This price they cannot, of course, assess, but it is revealed in their personalities and in their institutions. The very word "institutions," from my side of the ocean, where, it seemed to me, we suffered so cruelly from the lack of them, had a pleasant ring, as of safety and order and common sense; one had to come into contact with these institutions in order to understand that they were also outmoded, exasperating, completely impersonal, and very often cruel. Similarly, the personality which had seemed from a distance to be so large and free had to be dealt with before one could see that, if it was large, it was also inflexible and, for the foreigner, full of strange, high, dusty rooms which could not be inhabited. One had, in short, to come into contact with an alien culture in order to understand that a culture was not a community basket-weaving project, nor yet an act of God; was something neither desirable nor undesirable in itself, being inevitable, being nothing more or less than the recorded and visible effects on a body of people of the vicissitudes with which they had been forced to deal. And their great men are revealed as simply another of these vicissitudes, even if, quite against their will, the brief battle of their great men with them has left them richer.

When my American friend left his hotel to move to mine, he took with him, out of pique, a bedsheet belonging to the hotel and put it in his suitcase. When he arrived at my hotel I borrowed the sheet, since my own were filthy and the chambermaid showed no sign of bringing me any clean ones, and put it on my bed. The sheets belonging to *my* hotel I put out in the hall, congratulating myself on having thus forced on the attention of the Grand Hôtel du Bac the unpleasant state of its linen. Thereafter, since, as it turned out, we kept very different hours—I got up at noon, when, as I gathered by meeting him on the stairs one day, he was only just getting in—my new-found friend and I saw very little of each other.

On the evening of the 19th I was sitting thinking melancholy thoughts about Christmas and staring at the walls of my room. I imagine that I had sold something or that someone had sent me a Christmas present, for I remember that I had a little money. In those days in Paris, though I floated, so to speak, on a sea of acquaintances, I knew almost no one. Many people were eliminated from my orbit by virtue of the fact that they had more money than I did, which placed me, in my own eyes, in the humiliating role of a free-loader; and other people were eliminated by virtue of the fact that they enjoyed their poverty, shrilly insisting that this wretched round of hotel rooms, bad food, humiliating concierges, and unpaid bills was the Great Adventure. It couldn't, however, for me, end soon enough, this Great Adventure; there was a real question in my mind as to which would end soonest, the Great Adventure or me. This meant, however, that there were many evenings when I sat in my room, knowing that I couldn't work there, and not knowing what to do, or whom to see. On this particular evening I went down and knocked on the American's door.

There were two Frenchmen standing in the room, who immediately introduced themselves to me as policemen; which did not worry me. I had got used to policemen in Paris bobbing up at the most improbable times and places, asking to see one's *carte d'identité*. These policemen, however, showed very little interest in my papers. They were looking for something else. I could not imagine what this would be and, since I knew I certainly didn't have it, I scarcely followed the conversation they were having with my friend. I gathered that they were looking for some kind of gangster and since I wasn't a gangster and knew that gangsterism was not, insofar as he had one, my friend's style, I was sure that the two policemen would presently bow and say *Merci, messieurs*, and leave. For by this time, I remember very clearly, I was dying to have a drink and go to dinner.

I did not have a drink or go to dinner for many days after this, and when I did my outraged stomach promptly heaved everything up again. For now one of the policemen began to exhibit the most vivid interest in me and asked, very politely, if he might see my room. To which we mounted, making, I remember, the most civilized small talk on the way and even continuing it for some moments after we were in the room in which there was certainly nothing to be seen but the familiar poverty and disorder of that precarious group of people of whatever age, race, country, calling, or intention which Paris recognizes as *les étudiants* and sometimes, more ironically and precisely, as *les nonconformistes*. Then he moved to my bed, and in a terrible flash, not quite an instant before he lifted the bedspread, I understood what he was looking for. We looked at the sheet, on which I read, for the first time, lettered in the most brilliant scarlet I have ever seen, the name of the hotel from which it had been stolen. It was the first time the word *stolen* entered my mind. I had certainly seen the hotel monogram the day I put the sheet on the bed. It had simply meant nothing to me. In New York I had seen hotel monograms on everything from silver to soap and towels. Taking things from New York hotels was practically a custom, though, I suddenly realized, I had never known anyone to take a *sheet*. Sadly, and without a word to me, the inspector took the sheet from the bed, folded it under his arm, and we started back downstairs. I understood that I was under arrest.

And so we passed through the lobby, four of us, two of us very clearly criminal, under the eyes of the old man and his daughter, neither of whom said a word, into the streets where a light rain was falling. And I asked, in French, "But is this very serious?"

For I was thinking, it is, after all, only a sheet, not even new.

"No," said one of them. "It's not serious."

"It's nothing at all," said the other.

I took this to mean that we would receive a reprimand at the police station and be allowed to go to dinner. Later on I concluded that they were not being hypocritical or even trying to comfort us. They meant exactly what they said. It was only that they spoke another language.

In Paris everything is very slow. Also, when dealing with the bureaucracy, the man you are talking to is never the man you have to see. The man you have to see has just gone off to Belgium, or is busy with his family, or has just discovered that he is a cuckold; he will be in next Tuesday at three o'clock, or sometime in the course of the afternoon, or possibly tomorrow, or, possibly, in the next five minutes. But if he is coming in the next five minutes he will be far too busy to be able to see you today. So that I suppose I was not really astonished to learn at the commissariat that nothing could possibly be done about us before The Man arrived in the morning. But no, we could not go off and have dinner and come back in the morning. Of course he knew that we *would* come back—that was not the question. Indeed, there was no question: we would simply have to stay there for the night. We were placed in a cell which rather resembled a chicken coop. It was now about seven in the evening and I relinquished the thought of dinner and began to think of lunch.

I discouraged the chatter of my New York friend and this left me alone with my thoughts. I was beginning to be frightened and I bent all my energies, therefore, to keeping my panic under control. I began to realize that I was in a country I knew nothing about, in the hands of a people I did not understand at all. In a similar situation in New York I would have had some idea of what to do because I would have had some idea of what to expect. I am not speaking now of legality which, like most of the poor, I had never for an instant trusted, but of the temperament of the people with whom I had to deal. I had become very accomplished in New York at guessing and, therefore, to a limited extent manipulating to my advantage the reactions of the white world. But this was not New York. None of my old weapons could serve me here. I did not know what they saw when they looked at me. I knew very well what Americans saw when they looked at me and this allowed me to play endless and sinister variations on the role which they had assigned me; since I knew that it was, for them, of the utmost importance that they never be confronted with what, in their own personalities, made this role so necessary and gratifying to them, I knew that they could never call my hand or, indeed, afford to know what I was doing; so that I moved into every crucial situation with the deadly and rather desperate advantages of bitterly accumulated perception, of pride and contempt. This is an awful sword and shield to carry through the world, and the discovery that, in the game I was playing, I did myself a violence of which the world, at its most ferocious, would scarcely have been capable, was what had driven me out of New York. It was a strange feeling, in this situation, after a year in Paris, to discover that my weapons would never again serve me as they had.

It was quite clear to me that the Frenchmen in whose hands I found myself were no better or

worse than their American counterparts. Certainly
their uniforms frightened me quite as much, and
their impersonality, and the threat, always very
keenly felt by the poor, of violence, was as present
in that commissariat as it had ever been for me in
any police station. And I had seen, for example,
what Paris policemen could do to Arab peanut
vendors. The only difference here was that I did not
understand these people, did not know what techniques their cruelty took, did not know enough
about their personalities to see danger coming,
to ward it off, did not know on what ground to
meet it. That evening in the commissariat I was
not a despised black man. They would simply have
laughed at me if I had behaved like one. For them,
I was an American. And here it was they who had
the advantage, for that word, *Américain*, gave them
some idea, far from inaccurate, of what to expect from me. In order to corroborate none of
their ironical expectations I said nothing and did

nothing—which was not the way any Frenchman, white or black, would have reacted. The question thrusting up from the bottom of my mind was not *what* I was, but *who*. And this question, since a *what* can get by with skill but a *who* demands resources, was my first real intimation of what humility must mean.

In the morning it was still raining. Between nine and ten o'clock a black Citroën took us off to the Ile de la Cité, to the great, gray Préfecture. I realize now that the questions I put to the various policemen who escorted us were always answered in such a way as to corroborate what I wished to hear. This was not out of politeness, but simply out of indifference—or, possibly, an ironical pity— since each of the policemen knew very well that nothing would speed or halt the machine in which I had become entangled. They knew I did not know this and there was certainly no point in their telling me. In one way or another I would certainly come out at the other side—for they also knew that being found with a stolen bedsheet in one's possession was not a crime punishable by the guillotine. (They had the advantage over me there, too, for there were certainly moments later on when I was not so sure.) If I did *not* come out at the other side—well, that was just too bad. So, to my question, put while we were in the Citroën—"Will it be over today?"—I received a "*Oui, bien sûr*." He was not lying. As it turned out, the *procès-verbal* was over that day. Trying to be realistic, I dismissed, in the Citroën, all thoughts of lunch and pushed my mind ahead to dinner.

At the Préfecture we were first placed in a tiny cell, in which it was almost impossible either to sit or to lie down. After a couple of hours of this we were taken down to an office, where, for the first time, I encountered the owner of the bedsheet and where the *procès-verbal* took place. This was simply an interrogation, quite chillingly clipped and efficient (so that there was, shortly, no doubt in one's own mind that one *should* be treated as a criminal), which was recorded by a secretary. When it was over, this report was given to us to sign. One had, of course, no choice but to sign it, even though my mastery of written French was very far from certain. We were being held, according to the law in France, incommunicado, and all my angry demands to be allowed to speak to my embassy or to see a lawyer met with a stony *"Oui, oui. Plus tard."* The *procès-verbal* over, we were taken back to the cell, before which, shortly, passed the owner of the bedsheet. He said he hoped we had slept well, gave a vindictive wink, and disappeared.

By this time there was only one thing clear: that we had no way of controlling the sequence of events and could not possibly guess what this sequence would be. It seemed to me, since what I regarded as the high point—the *procès-verbal*—had been passed and since the hotel-keeper was once again in possession of his sheet, that we might reasonably expect to be released from police custody in a matter of hours. We had been detained now for what would soon be twenty-four hours, during which time I had learned only that the official charge against me was *receleur*. My mental shifting, between lunch and dinner, to say nothing of the physical lack of either of these delights, was beginning to make me dizzy. The steady chatter of my friend from New York, who was determined to keep my spirits up, made me feel murderous; I was praying that some power would release us from this freezing pile of stone before the impulse became the act. And I was beginning to wonder what was happening in that beautiful city, Paris, which lived outside these walls. I wondered how long it would take before anyone casually asked, "But where's Jimmy? He hasn't been around"— and realized, knowing the people I knew, that it would take several days.

Quite late in the afternoon we were taken from our cells; handcuffed, each to a separate officer; led through a maze of steps and corridors to the top of the building; fingerprinted; photographed. As in movies I had seen, I was placed against a wall, facing an old-fashioned camera, behind which stood one of the most completely cruel and indifferent faces I had ever seen, while someone next to me and, therefore, just outside my line of vision, read off in a voice from which all human feeling, even feeling of the most base description, had long since fled, what must be called my public characteristics—which, at that time and in that place, seemed anything but that. He might have been roaring to the hostile world secrets which I could barely, in the privacy of midnight, utter to myself. But he was only reading off my height, my features, my approximate weight, my color—that color which, in the United States, had often, odd as it may sound, been my salvation—the color of my hair, my age, my nationality. A light then flashed, the photographer and I staring at each other as though there was murder in our hearts, and then it was over. Handcuffed again, I was led downstairs to the bottom of the building, into a great enclosed shed in which had been gathered the very scrapings off the Paris streets. Old, old men, so ruined and old that life in them seemed really to prove the miracle of the quickening power of the Holy Ghost—for clearly their life was no longer their affair, it was no longer even their burden, they were simply the clay which had once been touched. And men not so old, with faces the color of lead and the consistency of oatmeal, eyes that made me think of stale *café-au-lait* spiked with arsenic, bodies which could take in food and water—any food and water—and pass it out, but which could not do anything more, except possibly, at midnight, along the riverbank where rats scurried, rape. And young men, harder and crueler than the Paris stones, older by far than I, their chronological senior by some five to seven years. And North Africans, old and young, who seemed the only living people in this place because they yet retained the grace to be bewildered. But they were not bewildered by being in this shed: they were simply bewildered because they were no longer in North Africa. There was a great hole in the center of this shed, which was the common toilet. Near it, though it was impossible to get very far from it, stood an old man with white hair, eating a piece of camembert. It was at this point, probably, that thought, for me, stopped, that physiology, if one may say so, took over. I found myself incapable of saying a word, not because I was afraid I would cry but because I was afraid I would vomit. And I did not think any longer of the city of Paris but my mind flew back to that home from which I had fled. I was sure that I would never see it any more. And it must have seemed to me that my flight from home was the cruelest trick I had ever played on myself, since it had led me here, down to a lower point than any I could ever in my life have imagined—lower, far, than anything I had seen in that Harlem which I had so hated and so loved, the escape from which had soon become the greatest direction of my life. After we had been here an hour or so a functionary came and opened the door and called out our names. And I was sure that *this* was my release. But I was handcuffed again and led out of the Préfecture into the streets—it was dark now, it was still raining—and before the steps of the Préfecture stood the great police wagon, doors facing me, wide open. The handcuffs were taken off, I entered the wagon, which was peculiarly constructed. It was divided by a narrow aisle, and on each side of the aisle was a series of narrow doors. These doors opened on a narrow cubicle, beyond which was a door which opened onto an-other narrow cubicle: three or four cubicles, each private, with a locking door. I was placed in one of them; I remember there was a small vent just above my head which let in a little light. The door of my cubicle was locked from the outside. I had no idea where this wagon was taking me and, as it began to move, I began to cry. I suppose I cried all the way to prison, the prison called Fresnes, which is twelve kilometers outside of Paris.

For reasons I have no way at all of understanding, prisoners whose last initial is A, B, or C are always sent to Fresnes; everybody else is sent to a prison called, rather cynically it seems to me, La Santé. I will, obviously, never be allowed to enter La Santé, but I was told by people who certainly seemed to know that it was infinitely more unbearable than Fresnes. This arouses in me, until today, a positive storm of curiosity concerning what I promptly began to think of as The Other Prison. My colleague in crime, occurring lower in the alphabet, had been sent there and I confess that the minute he was gone I missed him. I missed him because he was not French and because he was the only person in the world who knew that the story I told was true.

For, once locked in, divested of shoelaces, belt, watch, money, papers, nailfile, in a freezing cell in which both the window and the toilet were broken, with six other adventures, the story I told of *l'affaire du drap de lit* elicited only the wildest amusement or the most suspicious disbelief. Among the people who shared my cell the first three days no one, it is true, had been arrested for anything much more serious—or, at least, not serious in my eyes. I remember that there was a boy who had stolen a knitted sweater from a *monoprix*, who would probably, it was agreed, receive a six-month sentence. There was an older man there who had been arrested for some kind of petty larceny. There were two North Africans, vivid, brutish, and beautiful, who alternated between gaiety and fury, not at the fact of their arrest but at the state of the cell. None poured as much emotional energy into the fact of their arrest as I did; they took it, as I would have liked to take it, as simply another unlucky happening in a very dirty world. For, though I had grown accustomed to thinking of myself as looking upon the world with a hard, penetrating eye, the truth was that they were far more realistic about the world than I, and more nearly right about it. The gap between us, which only a gesture I made could have bridged, grew steadily, during thirty-six hours, wider. I could not make any gesture simply because they frightened me. I was unable to accept my imprisonment as a fact, even as a temporary fact. I could not, even for a moment, accept my present companions as *my* companions. And they, of course, felt this and put it down, with perfect justice, to the fact that I was an American.

There was nothing to do all day long. It appeared that we would one day come to trial but no one knew when. We were awakened at seven-thirty by a rapping on what I believe is called the Judas, that small opening in the door of the cell which allows the guards to survey the prisoners. At this rapping we rose from the floor—we slept on straw pallets and each of us was covered with one thin blanket—and moved to the door of the cell. We peered through the opening into the center of the prison, which was, as I remember, three tiers high, all gray stone and gunmetal steel, precisely that prison I had seen in movies, except that, in the movies, I had not known that it was cold in prison. I had not known that when one's shoelaces and belt have been removed one is, in the strangest way, demoralized. The necessity of shuffling and the necessity of holding up one's trousers with one hand turn one into a rag doll. And the movies fail, of course, to give one any idea of what prison food is like. Along the corridor, at seven-thirty, came three men, each pushing before him a great garbage can, mounted on wheels. In the garbage can of the first was the bread—this was passed to one through the small opening in the door. In the can of the second was the coffee. In the can of the third was what was always called *la soupe*, a pallid paste of potatoes which had certainly been bubbling on the back of the prison stove long before that first, so momentous revolution. Naturally, it was cold by this time and, starving as I was, I could not eat it. I drank the coffee—which was not coffee—because it was hot, and spent the rest of the day, huddled in my blanket, munching on the bread. It was not the French bread one bought in bakeries. In the evening the same procession returned. At ten-thirty the lights went out. I had a recurring dream, each night, a nightmare which always involved my mother's fried chicken. At the moment I was about to eat it came the rapping at the door. Silence is really all I remember of those first three days, silence and the color gray.

I am not sure now whether it was on the third or the fourth day that I was taken to trial for the first time. The days had nothing, obviously, to distinguish them from one another. I remember that I was very much aware that Christmas Day was approaching and I wondered if I was really going to spend Christmas Day in prison. And I remember that the first trial came the day before Christmas Eve.

On the morning of the first trial I was awakened by hearing my name called. I was told, hanging in a kind of void between my mother's fried chicken and the cold prison floor, "*Vous préparez. Vous êtes extrait*"—which simply terrified me, since I did not know what interpretation to put on the word "*extrait*," and since my cellmates had been amusing themselves with me by telling terrible stories about the inefficiency of French prisons, an inefficiency so extreme that it had often happened that someone who was supposed to be taken out and tried found himself on the wrong line and was guillotined instead. The best way of putting my reaction to this is to say that, though I knew they were teasing me, it was simply not possible for me to totally *dis*believe them. As far as I was concerned, once in the hands of the law in France, anything could happen. I shuffled along with the others who were *extrait* to the center of the prison, trying, rather, to linger in the office, which seemed the only warm spot in the whole world, and found myself again in that dreadful wagon, and was carried again to the Ile de la Cité, this time to the Palais de Justice. The entire day, except for ten minutes, was spent in one of the cells, first waiting to be tried, then waiting to be taken back to prison.

For I was *not* tried that day. By and by I was handcuffed and led through the halls, upstairs to the courtroom where I found my New York friend. We were placed together, both stage-whisperingly certain that this was the end of our ordeal. Nevertheless, while I waited for our case to be called, my eyes searched the courtroom, looking for a face I knew, hoping, anyway, that there was someone there who knew *me*, who would carry to someone outside the news that I was in trouble. But there was no one I knew there and I had had time to realize that there was probably only one man in Paris who could help me, an American patent attorney for whom I had worked as an office boy. He could have helped me because he had a quite solid position and some prestige and would have testified that, while working for him, I had handled large sums of money regularly, which made it rather unlikely that I would stoop to trafficking in bedsheets. However, he was somewhere in Paris, probably at this very moment enjoying a snack and a glass of wine and as far as the possibility of reaching him was concerned, he might as well have been on Mars. I tried to watch the proceedings and to make my mind a blank. But the proceedings were not reassuring. The boy, for example, who had stolen the sweater *did* receive a six-month sentence. It seemed to me that all the sentences meted out that day were excessive; though, again, it seemed that all the people who were sentenced that day had made, or clearly were going to make, crime their career. This seemed to be the opinion of the judge, who scarcely looked at the prisoners or listened to them; it seemed to be the opinion of the prisoners, who scarcely bothered to speak in their own behalf; it seemed to be the opinion of the lawyers, state lawyers for the most part, who were defending them. The great impulse of the courtroom seemed to be to put these people where they could not be seen——and not because they were offended at the crimes, unless, indeed, they were offended that the crimes were so petty, but because they did not wish to know that their society could be counted on to produce, probably in greater and greater numbers, a whole body of people for whom crime was the only possible career. Any society inevitably produces its criminals, but a society at once rigid and unstable can do nothing whatever to alleviate the poverty of its lowest members, cannot present to the hypothetical young man at the crucial moment that so-well-advertised right path. And the fact, perhaps, that the French are the earth's least sentimental people and must also be numbered among the most proud aggravates the plight of their lowest, youngest, and unluckiest members, for it means that the idea of rehabilitation is scarcely real to them. I confess that this attitude on their part raises in me sentiments of exasperation, admiration, and despair, revealing as it does, in both the best and the worst sense, their renowned and spectacular hard-headedness.

Finally our case was called and we rose. We gave our names. At the point that it developed that we were American the proceedings ceased, a hurried consultation took place between the judge and what I took to be several lawyers. Someone called out for an interpreter. The arresting officer had forgotten to mention our nationalities and there was, therefore, no interpreter in the court. Even if our French had been better than it was we would not have been allowed to stand trial without an interpreter. Before I clearly understood what was happening, I was handcuffed again and led out of the courtroom. The trial had been set back for the 27th of December.

I have sometimes wondered if I would *ever* have got out of prison if it had not been for the older man who had been arrested for the mysterious petty larceny. He was acquitted that day and when he returned to the cell—for he could not be released until morning—he found me sitting numbly on the floor, having just been prevented, by the sight of a man, all blood, being carried back to *his* cell on a stretcher, from seizing the bars and screaming until they let me out. The sight of the man on the stretcher proved, however, that screaming would not do much for me. The petty-larceny man went around asking if he could do anything in the world outside for those he was leaving behind. When he came to me I, at first, responded, "No, nothing"——for I suppose I had by now retreated into the attitude, the earliest I remember, that of my father, which was simply (since I had lost his God) that nothing could help me. And I suppose I will remember with gratitude until I die the fact that the man now insisted: "*Mais, êtes-vous sûr?*" Then it swept over me that he was going *outside* and he instantly became my first contact since the Lord alone knew how long with the outside world. At the same time, I remember, I did not really believe that he would help me. There was no reason why he should. But I gave him the phone number of my attorney friend and my own name.

So, in the middle of the next day, Christmas Eve, I shuffled downstairs again, to meet my visitor. He looked extremely well fed and sane and clean. He told me I had nothing to worry about any more. Only not even he could do anything to make the mill of justice grind any faster. He would, however, send me a lawyer of his acquaintance who would defend me on the 27th, and he would himself, along with several other people, appear as a character witness. He gave me a package of Lucky Strikes (which the turnkey took from me on the way upstairs) and said that, though it was doubtful that there would be any celebration in the prison, he would see to it that I got a fine Christmas dinner when I got out. And this, somehow, seemed very funny. I remember being astonished at the discovery that I was actually laughing. I was, too, I imagine, also rather disappointed that my hair had not turned white, that my face was clearly not going to bear any marks of tragedy, disappointed at bottom, no doubt, to realize, facing him in that room, that far worse things had happened to most people and that, indeed, to paraphrase my mother, if this was the worst thing that ever happened to me I could consider myself among the luckiest people ever to be born. He injected—my visitor—into my solitary nightmare common sense, the world, and the hint of blacker things to come.

The next day, Christmas, unable to endure my cell, and feeling that, after all, the day demanded a gesture, I asked to be allowed to go to Mass, hoping to hear some music. But I found myself, for a freezing hour and a half, locked in exactly the same kind of cubicle as in the wagon which had first brought me to prison, peering through a slot placed at the level of the eye at an old Frenchman, hatted, overcoated, muffled, and gloved, preaching in this language which I did not understand, to this row of wooden boxes, the story of Jesus Christ's love for men.

The next day, the 26th, I spent learning a peculiar kind of game, played with match-sticks, with my cellmates. For, since I no longer felt that I would stay in this cell forever, I was beginning to be able to make peace with it for a time. On the 27th I went again to trial and, as had been predicted, the case against us was dismissed. The story of the *drap de lit*, finally told, caused great merriment in the courtroom, whereupon my friend decided that the French were "great." I was chilled by their merriment, even though it was meant to warm me. It could only remind me of the laughter I had often heard at home, laughter which I had sometimes deliberately elicited. This laughter is the laughter of those who consider themselves to be at a safe remove from all the wretched, for whom the pain of the living is not real. I had heard it so often in my native land that I had resolved to find a place where I would never hear it any more. In some deep, black, stony, and liberating way, my life, in my own eyes, began during that first year in Paris, when it was borne in on me that this laughter is universal and never can be stilled.

STRANGER IN
THE VILLAGE

FROM ALL AVAILABLE evidence no black man
had ever set foot in this tiny Swiss village before
I came. I was told before arriving that I would
probably be a "sight" for the village; I took this to
mean that people of my complexion were rarely
seen in Switzerland, and also that city people are
always something of a "sight" outside of the city.
It did not occur to me—possibly because I am an
American—that there could be people anywhere
who had never seen a Negro.

It is a fact that cannot be explained on the basis of the inaccessibility of the village. The village is very high, but it is only four hours from Milan and three hours from Lausanne. It is true that it is virtually unknown. Few people making plans for a holiday would elect to come here. On the other hand, the villagers are able, presumably, to come and go as they please—which they do: to another town at the foot of the mountain, with a population of approximately five thousand, the nearest place to see a movie or go to the bank. In the village there is no movie house, no bank, no library, no theater; very few radios, one jeep, one station wagon; and, at the moment, one typewriter, mine, an invention which the woman next door to me here had never seen. There are about six hundred people living here, all Catholic—I conclude this from the fact that the Catholic church is open all year round, whereas the Protestant chapel, set off on a hill a little removed from the village, is open only in the summertime

when the tourists arrive. There are four or five hotels, all closed now, and four or five *bistros*, of which,
however, only two do any business during the winter. These two do not do a great deal, for life in the
village seems to end around nine or ten o'clock.
There are a few stores, butcher, baker, *épicerie*, a
hardware store, and a money-changer—who cannot change travelers' checks, but must send them
down to the bank, an operation which takes two
or three days. There is something called the *Ballet
Haus*, closed in the winter and used for God knows
what, certainly not ballet, during the summer. There
seems to be only one schoolhouse in the village, and
this for the quite young children; I suppose this to
mean that their older brothers and sisters at some
point descend from these mountains in order to
complete their education—possibly, again, to the
town just below. The landscape is absolutely for-
bidding, mountains towering on all four sides, ice
and snow as far as the eye can reach. In this white

wilderness, men and women and children move all day, carrying washing, wood, buckets of milk or water, sometimes skiing on Sunday afternoons. All week long boys and young men are to be seen shoveling snow off the rooftops, or dragging wood down from the forest in sleds.

The village's only real attraction, which explains the tourist season, is the hot spring water. A disquietingly high proportion of these tourists are cripples, or semicripples, who come year after year—from other parts of Switzerland, usually—to take the waters. This lends the village, at the height of the season, a rather terrifying air of sanctity, as though it were a lesser Lourdes. There is often something beautiful, there is always something awful, in the spectacle of a person who has lost one of his faculties, a faculty he never questioned until it was gone, and who struggles to recover it. Yet people remain people, on crutches or indeed on deathbeds; and wherever I passed, the first summer I was here, among the native villagers or among the lame, a wind passed with me—of astonishment, curiosity, amusement, and outrage. That first summer I stayed two weeks and never intended to return. But I did return in the winter, to work; the village offers, obviously, no distractions whatever and has the further advantage of being extremely cheap. Now it is winter again, a year later, and I am here again. Everyone in the village knows my name, though they scarcely ever use it, knows that I come from America—though, this, apparently, they will never really believe: black men come from Africa—and everyone knows that I am the friend of the son of a woman who was born here, and that I am staying in their chalet. But I remain as much a stranger today as I was the first day I arrived, and the children shout *Neger! Neger!* as I walk along the streets.

It must be admitted that in the beginning I was far too shocked to have any real reaction. In so far as

I reacted at all, I reacted by trying to be pleasant—
it being a great part of the American Negro's education (long before he goes to school) that he must
make people "like" him. This smile-and-the-world-
smiles-with-you routine worked about as well in
this situation as it had in the situation for which
it was designed, which is to say that it did not
work at all. No one, after all, can be liked whose
human weight and complexity cannot be, or has
not been, admitted. My smile was simply another
unheard-of phenomenon which allowed them to
see my teeth—they did not, really, see my smile
and I began to think that, should I take to snarl-
ing, no one would notice any difference. All of
the physical characteristics of the Negro which
had caused me, in America, a very different and
almost forgotten pain were nothing less than mi-
raculous—or infernal—in the eyes of the village
people. Some thought my hair was the color of tar,
that it had the texture of wire, or the texture of

cotton. It was jocularly suggested that I might let it all grow long and make myself a winter coat. If I sat in the sun for more than five minutes some daring creature was certain to come along and gingerly put his fingers on my hair, as though he were afraid of an electric shock, or put his hand on my hand, astonished that the color did not rub off. In all of this, in which it must be conceded there was the charm of genuine wonder and in which there was certainly no element of intentional unkindness, there was yet no suggestion that I was human: I was simply a living wonder.

I knew that they did not mean to be unkind, and I know it now; it is necessary, nevertheless, for me to repeat this to myself each time that I walk out of the chalet. The children who shout *Neger!* have no way of knowing the echoes this sound raises in me. They are brimming with good humor and the more daring swell with pride when I stop to speak with them. Just the same, there are days when I cannot pause and smile, when I have no heart to play with them; when, indeed, I mutter sourly to myself, exactly as I muttered on the streets of a city these children have never seen, when I was no bigger than these children are now: *Your* mother *was a nigger*. Joyce is right about history being a nightmare—but it may be the nightmare from which no one *can* awaken. People are trapped in history and history is trapped in them.

There is a custom in the village—I am told it is repeated in many villages—of "buying" African natives for the purpose of converting them to Christianity. There stands in the church all year round a small box with a slot for money, decorated with a black figurine, and into this box the villagers drop their francs. During the *carnaval* which precedes Lent, two village children have their faces blackened—out of which bloodless darkness their blue eyes shine like ice—and fantastic horsehair wigs are placed on their blond heads;

thus disguised, they solicit among the villagers for money for the missionaries in Africa. Between the box in the church and the blackened children, the village "bought" last year six or eight African natives. This was reported to me with pride by the wife of one of the *bistro* owners and I was careful to express astonishment and pleasure at the solicitude shown by the village for the souls of black folk. The *bistro* owner's wife beamed with a pleasure far more genuine than my own and seemed to feel that I might now breathe more easily concerning the souls of at least six of my kinsmen.

I tried not to think of these so lately baptized kinsmen, of the price paid for them, or the peculiar price they themselves would pay, and said nothing about my father, who having taken his own conversion too literally never, at bottom, forgave the white world (which he described as heathen) for having saddled him with a Christ in whom, to judge at least from their treatment of him, they themselves no longer believed. I thought of white men arriving for the first time in an African village, strangers there, as I am a stranger here, and tried to imagine the astounded populace touching their hair and marveling at the color of their skin. But there is a great difference between being the first white man to be seen by Africans and being the first black man to be seen by whites. The white man takes the astonishment as tribute, for he arrives to conquer and to convert the natives, whose inferiority in relation to himself is not even to be questioned; whereas I, without a thought of conquest, find myself among a people whose culture controls me, has even, in a sense, created me, people who have cost me more in anguish and rage than they will ever know, who yet do not even know of my existence. The astonishment with which I might have greeted them, should they have stumbled into my African village a few hundred years ago, might have rejoiced their hearts. But the astonishment with which they greet me today can only poison mine.

And this is so despite everything I may do to feel differently, despite my friendly conversations with the *bistro* owner's wife, despite their three-year-old son who has at last become my friend, despite the *saluts* and *bonsoirs* which I exchange with people as I walk, despite the fact that I know that no individual can be taken to task for what history is doing, or has done. I say that the culture of these people controls me—but they can scarcely be held responsible for European culture. America comes out of Europe, but these people have never seen America, nor have most of them seen more of Europe than the hamlet at the foot of their mountain. Yet they move with an authority which I shall never have; and they regard me, quite rightly, not only as a stranger in their village but as a suspect latecomer, bearing no credentials, to everything they have—however unconsciously—inherited.

For this village, even were it incomparably more remote and incredibly more primitive, is the West, the West onto which I have been so strangely grafted. These people cannot be, from the point of view of power, strangers anywhere in the world; they have made the modern world, in effect, even if they do not know it. The most illiterate among them is related, in a way that I am not, to Dante, Shakespeare, Michelangelo, Aeschylus, Da Vinci, Rembrandt, and Racine; the cathedral at Chartres says something to them which it cannot say to me, as indeed would New York's Empire State Building, should anyone here ever see it. Out of their hymns and dances come Beethoven and Bach. Go back a few centuries and they are in their full glory—but I am in Africa, watching the conquerors arrive.

The rage of the disesteemed is personally fruitless, but it is also absolutely inevitable; this rage, so generally discounted, so little understood even among the people whose daily bread it is, is one of the things that makes history. Rage can only with difficulty, and never entirely, be brought under the domination of the intelligence and is therefore not susceptible to any arguments whatever. This is a fact which ordinary representatives of the *Herrenvolk*, having never felt this rage and being unable to imagine it, quite fail to understand. Also, rage cannot be hidden, it can only be dissembled. This dissembling deludes the thoughtless, and strengthens rage and adds, to rage, contempt. There are, no doubt, as many ways of coping with the resulting complex of tensions as there are black men in the world, but no black man can hope ever to be entirely liberated from this internal warfare—rage, dissembling, and contempt having inevitably accompanied his first realization of the power of white men. What is crucial here is that, since white men represent in the black man's world so heavy a weight, white men have for black men a reality which is far from being reciprocal; and hence all black men have toward all white men an attitude which is designed, really, either to rob the white man of the jewel of his naïveté, or else to make it cost him dear.

The black man insists, by whatever means he finds at his disposal, that the white man cease to regard him as an exotic rarity and recognize him as a human being. This is a very charged and difficult moment, for there is a great deal of will power involved in the white man's naïveté. Most people are not naturally reflective any more than they are naturally malicious, and the white man prefers to keep the black man at a certain human remove because it is easier for him thus to preserve his simplicity and avoid being called to account for crimes committed by his forefathers, or his neighbors. He is inescapably aware, nevertheless, that he is in a better position in the world than black men are, nor can he quite put to death the suspicion that he is hated by black men therefore. He does not wish to be hated, neither does he wish to change places, and at this point in his uneasiness he can scarcely avoid having recourse to those legends which white men have created about black men, the most usual effect of which is that the white man finds himself enmeshed, so to speak, in his own language which describes hell, as well as the attributes which lead one to hell, as being as black as night.

Every legend, moreover, contains its residuum of truth, and the root function of language is to control the universe by describing it. It is of quite considerable significance that black men remain, in the imagination, and in overwhelming numbers in fact, beyond the disciplines of salvation; and this despite the fact that the West has been "buying" African natives for centuries. There is, I should hazard, an instantaneous necessity to be divorced from this so visibly unsaved stranger, in whose heart, moreover, one cannot guess what dreams of vengeance are being nourished; and, at the same time, there are few things on earth more attractive than the idea of the unspeakable liberty which is allowed the unredeemed. When, beneath the black mask, a human being begins to make himself felt one cannot escape a certain awful wonder as to what kind of human being it is. What one's imagination makes of other people is dictated, of course, by the laws of one's own personality and it is one of the ironies of black-white relations that, by means of what the white man imagines the black man to be, the black man is enabled to know who the white man is.

I have said, for example, that I am as much a stranger in this village today as I was the first summer I arrived, but this is not quite true. The villagers wonder less about the texture of my hair than they did then, and wonder rather more about me. And the fact that their wonder now exists on another level is reflected in their attitudes and in their eyes. There are the children who make those delightful, hilarious, sometimes astonishingly grave overtures of friendship in the unpredictable fashion of children; other children, having been taught that the devil is a black man, scream in genuine anguish as I approach. Some of the older women never pass without a friendly greeting, never pass, indeed, if it seems that they will be able to engage me in conversation; other women look down or look away or rather contemptuously smirk. Some of the men drink with me and suggest that I learn how to ski—partly, I gather, because they cannot imagine what I would look like on skis—and want to know if I am married, and ask questions about my *métier*. But some of the men have accused *le sale nègre*—behind my back—of stealing wood and there is already in the eyes of some of them that peculiar, intent, paranoiac malevolence which one sometimes surprises in the eyes of American white men when, out walking with their Sunday girl, they see a Negro male approach.

There is a dreadful abyss between the streets of this village and the streets of the city in which I was born, between the children who shout *Neger!* today and those who shouted *Nigger!* yesterday—the abyss is experience, the American experience. The syllable hurled behind me today expresses, above all, wonder: I am a stranger here. But I am not a stranger in America and the same syllable riding on the American air expresses the war my presence has occasioned in the American soul.

For this village brings home to me this fact: that there was a day, and not really a very distant day, when Americans were scarcely Americans at all but discontented Europeans, facing a great unconquered continent and strolling, say, into a marketplace and seeing black men for the first time. The shock this spectacle afforded is suggested, surely, by the promptness with which they decided that these black men were not really men but cattle. It is true that the necessity on the part of the settlers of the New World of reconciling their moral assumptions with the fact—and the necessity—of slavery enhanced immensely the charm of this idea, and it is also true that this idea expresses, with a truly American bluntness, the attitude which to varying extents all masters have had toward all slaves.

But between all former slaves and slave-owners and the drama which begins for Americans over three hundred years ago at Jamestown, there are at least two differences to be observed. The American Negro slave could not suppose, for one thing, as slaves in past epochs had supposed and often done, that he would ever be able to wrest the power from his master's hands. This was a supposition which the modern era, which was to bring about such vast changes in the aims and dimensions of

power, put to death; it only begins, in unprecedented fashion, and with dreadful implications, to
be resurrected today. But even had this supposition
persisted with undiminished force, the American
Negro slave could not have used it to lend his con-
dition dignity, for the reason that this supposition
rests on another: that the slave in exile yet remains
related to his past, has some means—if only in
memory—of revering and sustaining the forms
of his former life, is able, in short, to maintain
his identity.

This was not the case with the American Negro slave. He is unique among the black men of
the world in that his past was taken from him,
almost literally, at one blow. One wonders what
on earth the first slave found to say to the first dark
child he bore. I am told that there are Haitians
able to trace their ancestry back to African kings,
but any American Negro wishing to go back so
far will find his journey through time abruptly

arrested by the signature on the bill of sale which served as the entrance paper for his ancestor. At the time—to say nothing of the circumstances— of the enslavement of the captive black man who was to become the American Negro, there was not the remotest possibility that he would ever take power from his master's hands. There was no reason to suppose that his situation would ever change, nor was there, shortly, anything to indicate that his situation had ever been different. It was his necessity, in the words of E. Franklin Frazier, to find a "motive for living under American culture or die." The identity of the American Negro comes out of this extreme situation, and the evolution of this identity was a source of the most intolerable anxiety in the minds and the lives of his masters.

For the history of the American Negro is unique also in this: that the question of his humanity, and of his rights therefore as a human being, became a burning one for several generations of

Americans, so burning a question that it ultimately became one of those used to divide the nation. It is out of this argument that the venom of the epithet *Nigger!* is derived. It is an argument which Europe has never had, and hence Europe quite sincerely fails to understand how or why the argument arose in the first place, why its effects are so frequently disastrous and always so unpredictable, why it refuses until today to be entirely settled. Europe's black possessions remained—and do remain—in Europe's colonies, at which remove they represented no threat whatever to European identity. If they posed any problem at all for the European conscience, it was a problem which remained comfortingly abstract: in effect, the black man, *as a man*, did not exist for Europe. But in America, even as a slave, he was an inescapable part of the general social fabric and no American could escape having an attitude toward him. Americans attempt until today to make an abstraction of the Negro, but the very nature of these abstractions reveals the tremendous effects the presence of the Negro has had on the American character.

When one considers the history of the Negro in America it is of the greatest importance to recognize that the moral beliefs of a person, or a people, are never really as tenuous as life—which is not moral—very often causes them to appear; these create for them a frame of reference and a necessary hope, the hope being that when life has done its worst they will be enabled to rise above themselves and to triumph over life. Life would scarcely be bearable if this hope did not exist. Again, even when the worst has been said, to betray a belief is not by any means to have put oneself beyond its power; the betrayal of a belief is not the same thing as ceasing to believe. If this were not so there would be no moral standards in the world at all. Yet one must also recognize that morality is based on ideas and that all ideas are dangerous—dangerous because ideas can only lead to action and where the action leads no man can say. And dangerous in this respect: that confronted with the impossibility of remaining faithful to one's beliefs, and the equal impossibility of becoming free of them, one can be driven to the most inhuman excesses. The ideas on which American beliefs are based are not, though Americans often seem to think so, ideas which originated in America. They came out of Europe. And the establishment of democracy on the American continent was scarcely as radical a break with the past as was the necessity, which Americans faced, of broadening this concept to include black men.

This was, literally, a hard necessity. It was impossible, for one thing, for Americans to abandon their beliefs, not only because these beliefs alone seemed able to justify the sacrifices they had endured and the blood that they had spilled, but also because these beliefs afforded them their only bulwark against a moral chaos as absolute as the physical chaos of the continent it was their destiny to conquer. But in the situation in which Americans found themselves, these beliefs threatened an idea which, whether or not one likes to think so, is the very warp and woof of the heritage of the West, the idea of white supremacy.

Americans have made themselves notorious by the shrillness and the brutality with which they have insisted on this idea, but they did not invent it; and it has escaped the world's notice that those very excesses of which Americans have been guilty imply a certain, unprecedented uneasiness over the idea's life and power, if not, indeed, the idea's validity. The idea of white supremacy rests simply on the fact that white men are the creators of civilization (the present civilization, which is the only one that matters; all previous civilizations are simply "contributions" to our own) and are therefore civilization's guardians and defenders.

Thus it was impossible for Americans to accept the black man as one of themselves, for to do so was to jeopardize their status as white men. But not so to accept him was to deny his human reality, his human weight and complexity, and the strain of denying the overwhelmingly undeniable forced Americans into rationalizations so fantastic that they approached the pathological.

At the root of the American Negro problem is the necessity of the American white man to find a way of living with the Negro in order to be able to live with himself. And the history of this problem can be reduced to the means used by Americans—lynch law and law, segregation and legal acceptance, terrorization and concession—either to come to terms with this necessity, or to find a way around it, or (most usually) to find a way of doing both these things at once. The resulting spectacle, at once foolish and dreadful, led someone to make the quite accurate observation that "the Negro-in-America is a form of insanity which overtakes white men."

In this long battle, a battle by no means finished, the unforeseeable effects of which will be felt by many future generations, the white man's motive was the protection of his identity; the black man was motivated by the need to establish an identity. And despite the terrorization which the Negro in America endured and endures sporadically until today, despite the cruel and totally inescapable ambivalence of his status in his country, the battle for his identity has long ago been won. He is not a visitor to the West, but a citizen there, an American; as American as the Americans who despise him, the Americans who fear him, the Americans who love him—the Americans who became less than themselves, or rose to be greater than themselves by virtue of the fact that the challenge he represented was inescapable. He is perhaps the only black man in the world whose relationship to white men is more terrible, more subtle, and more meaningful than the relationship of bitter possessed to uncertain possessor. His survival depended, and his development depends, on his ability to turn his peculiar status in the Western world to his own advantage and, it may be, to the very great advantage of that world. It remains for him to fashion out of his experience that which will give him sustenance, and a voice.

The cathedral at Chartres, I have said, says something to the people of this village which it cannot say to me; but it is important to understand that this cathedral says something to me which it cannot say to them. Perhaps they are struck by the power of the spires, the glory of the windows; but they have known God, after all, longer than I have known him, and in a different way, and I am terrified by the slippery bottomless well to be found in the crypt, down which heretics were hurled to death, and by the obscene, inescapable gargoyles jutting out of the stone and seeming to say that God and the devil can never be divorced. I doubt that the villagers think of the devil when they face a cathedral because they have never been identified with the devil. But I must accept the status which myth, if nothing else, gives me in the West before I can hope to change the myth.

Yet, if the American Negro has arrived at his identity by virtue of the absoluteness of his estrangement from his past, American white men still nourish the illusion that there is some means of recovering the European innocence, of returning to a state in which black men do not exist. This is one of the greatest errors Americans can make. The identity they fought so hard to protect has, by virtue of that battle, undergone a change: Americans are as unlike any other white people in the world as it is possible to be. I do not think, for example, that it is too much to suggest that the American vision of the world—which allows so little reality, generally speaking, for any of the darker forces in human life, which tends until today to paint moral issues in glaring black and white—owes a great deal to the battle waged by Americans to maintain between themselves and black men a human separation which could not be bridged. It is only now beginning to be borne in on us—very faintly, it must be admitted, very slowly, and very much against our will—that this vision of the world is dangerously inaccurate, and perfectly useless. For it protects our moral high-mindedness at the terrible expense of weakening our grasp of reality. People who shut their eyes to reality simply invite their own destruction, and anyone who insists on remaining in a state of innocence long after that innocence is dead turns himself into a monster.

The time has come to realize that the inter-racial drama acted out on the American continent has not only created a new black man, it has created a new white man, too. No road whatever will lead Americans back to the simplicity of this European village where white men still have the luxury of looking on me as a stranger. I am not, really, a stranger any longer for any American alive. One of the things that distinguishes Americans from other people is that no other people has ever been so deeply involved in the lives of black men, and vice versa. This fact faced, with all its implications, it can be seen that the history of the American Negro problem is not merely shameful, it is also something of an achievement. For even when the worst has been said, it must also be added that the perpetual challenge posed by this problem was always, somehow, perpetually met. It is precisely this black-white experience which may prove of indispensable value to us in the world we face today. This world is white no longer, and it will never be white again.

ABOUT
THE AUTHOR

J AMES BALDWIN (1924–1987) was a novelist, an
essayist, a playwright, a poet, and a social critic,
and one of America's foremost writers. His writing explores palpable yet unspoken intricacies of
racial, sexual, and class distinctions in Western
societies, most notably in mid-twentieth-century
America. A Harlem, New York, native, he lived
periodically in exile in the south of France and
in Turkey. He is the author of several novels and
books of nonfiction, including *Notes of a Native Son*,
Go Tell It on the Mountain, *Giovanni's Room*, *Another*

Country, Tell Me How Long the Train's Been Gone, If Beale Street Could Talk, Just Above My Head, The Fire Next Time, No Name in the Street, and *The Evidence of Things Not Seen,* and of the poetry collection *Jimmy's Blues.*